Visualization

An Intricate Guide To Utilizing Visualization Techniques

To Tap Into The Profound Potential Of Your

Subconscious Mind And A Comprehensive, Sequential

Manual

Leopoldo Trujillo

TABLE OF CONTENT

What is Visualization?

Visualization can be described as a cognitive or perceptual process of mentally rehearsing an event or situation. There is a tendency wherein individuals commonly construct mental representations or narratives depicting themselves engaging in or possessing desired outcomes within the realm of reality.

You repeatedly review these images or descriptions. In a brief interval of just five minutes, it implores you to envision yourself achieving remarkable success, emerging triumphant in business negotiations, fostering strong and harmonious connections, attaining optimal health, or manifesting any desired objectives you may wish to manifest.

It is essential to bear in mind that the mental imagery one generates should consistently harbor a strong inclination towards desiring the actualization of the envisioned outcome in one's own life. This phenomenon is commonly referred to as the cognitive manipulation. You refrain from engaging in wishful thinking, but rather cultivate the conviction that your desired outcome will inevitably materialize in the future.

Through the implementation of visualization exercises, one can experience the sensation of living in the present moment, as if the events are unfolding before their very eyes.

At a certain level of consciousness, one remains cognizant that this is merely a psychological illusion; however, the tangible reality we experience does not align with our perception. One crucial point to grasp is that the human subconscious is unable to discern between reality and imagination.

The operations of your subconscious mind are influenced by the descriptions or images that you construct within your own psyche, irrespective of their correspondence to the current reality.

You consistently draw towards yourself the things upon which you direct your attention. Although individuals may not consciously acknowledge these phenomena, they experience and perceive the oscillating energy that is influenced by their thoughts and cognitive processes. Our beliefs consistently endeavor to manifest themselves.

Our thoughts or convictions possess imaginative power, and upon recognizing them, we commence shaping our daily existence with heightened clarity and a more distinct sense of direction. We can leverage this reality to imbue greater meaning into our lives.

Each day, it is essential to dedicate your attention to your aspirations or desires. In addition, we present the utilization of Mind Power techniques to aid you in this matter. This system comprises a set of uncomplicated methodologies that enhance your ability to concentrate and channel your thoughts towards a lucid direction.

In this edition, we will delve into the various methods of visualization and explore their efficacy in unleashing our latent capabilities.

The Vision Board was ineffective in its outcomes.

If the assertions presented on the vision board did not yield the desired outcome, it may be attributed to your lack of conviction in their validity. The success or failure of your writing is determined by the workings of your mind, and it is possible that you are not employing sufficiently impactful language to effectively engage your own mind. Observe them and reflect upon whether this truly aligns with your aspirations for a fulfilling existence. Now, position the board in front of you within a serene environment, and dedicate daily intervals to its contemplation, persisting in the repetition of the written mantras. It is not possible to instantaneously transform a pessimistic mindset into a positive one, and it is necessary to consistently reinforce positive affirmations until one truly internalizes and embraces each word inscribed on these boards. Allow me to provide you with an excellent illustration of the potential consequences that may arise from taking such actions.

Cynthia Stafford successfully secured a staggering sum of $112 million through the utilization of the Law of Attraction in the lottery. She was enduring a profoundly challenging existence as she assumed responsibility for her brother's children after his passing. Throughout her YouTube video, she consistently emphasized the importance of envisioning oneself in a position of success, regardless of the desired goals in life. This purpose is precisely fulfilled by the utilization of vision boards. If one's conviction is sufficiently firm, circumstances can manifest, for it is contingent upon the magnitude of optimistic energy one possesses or imbues into their existence. Individuals with a proclivity towards exuberant energy tend to gravitate towards activities and endeavors that mirror and complement their dynamic disposition.

They also appeal to individuals of elevated enthusiasm and vigor.

Cynthia meticulously transcribed the precise sum of her triumph onto a sheet of paper, employing a mental image of her beloved progeny as a motivational catalyst that propelled her transformation from a struggling mother to the individual she has become in the present day. She could perceive the impact of this on the children, although she did not regard it as a venture with lasting implications. She observed the children deriving immediate benefits. There are others who also have stories to share. It is advisable for you to consider watching her story on YouTube, while also seeking out other narratives as they hold equal significance. This is not trivial and once you cease to have confidence in the content inscribed on the vision board, the aspiration vanishes. Therefore, it is imperative that you commence anew and genuinely embrace this belief. In order to truly transform into the person you aspire to be, it is essential to wholeheartedly embrace the conviction in your written words and vividly envision your existence embodying that persona.

Visualization encompasses the practice of closing one's eyes and conjuring mental imagery of one's existence and presence within the world. Similar to a child envisioning themselves as an astronaut, you envision yourself as the individual you aspire to become and authentically experience the emotions associated with that identity, for without this driving force, one's energy levels may not reach the required heights for accomplishment. The process of visualizing requires effort, but it is an indispensable endeavor in order to achieve one's desired destination.

Thanks to my unwavering faith in the efficacy of visualization, I have attained all that I have ever desired in my existence. No, I do not possess the highest wealth on the planet; however, attaining such opulence has never aligned with the aspirations I hold. I successfully attained a state of inner tranquility, contentment, and serenity by altering my mindset, aligning with my vision. A few years prior, I experienced a profound state of depression which had afflicted me persistently for an extended duration. In reality, individuals afflicted with depression often find themselves repeatedly seeking medical assistance due to the repetitive affirmation of their depressed state, such as identifying themselves as "depressed" or "a depressive individual." While it is acknowledged that not all instances are identical and it would be imprudent to make such a sweeping declaration, the underlying thought patterns within the human mind remain strikingly similar. Therefore, there exists a potential for personal transformation and the ability to alter one's core identity. I transitioned from a mindset of victimhood to taking charge of my life, assuming the role of a protagonist. As a result, I have reached a stage where all my desires in life seamlessly materialize due to the uplifting energy I am able to radiate. I hold a firm conviction in the principles underlying the Law of Attraction and will endeavor to elucidate its concept.

If one were to enter a ballroom with a sense of self-doubt regarding the appearance of their dress and the quality of their hairstyle, their energy levels or vibrations would be perceived as diminished. You have low expectations. At the utmost, you may potentially receive an invitation to partake in a dance from an individual who possesses unexceptional physical attractiveness, consequently not sought after by others. Why? It is unrelated to your physical appearance. It pertains to the emanations of vibrations that you emit. Now, if you were to adorn a girl endowed with self-assurance with the identical attire and hairstyle, she would not merely secure invitations to dance solely from individuals who have been overlooked by others. Therefore, it is neither the attire nor the hairstyle. It's the energy emitted.

Enter the dance venue exuding an aura of regality, embodying the demeanor and composure of a princess. Regardless of the opinions held by others regarding your attire, prioritize the essence of contentment and emanate an infectious sense of joy, thereby attracting a similarly positive atmosphere. Gentlemen will take notice of your presence, and it is absolutely not attributable to your attire. The reason behind your appeal to confident and joyful individuals is the emanation of these qualities that you exhibit, which in turn attracts the attention and desire of desirable suitors who wish to engage in dancing with you. Energy is paramount, and the practice of visualization can serve as a valuable tool to harness and cultivate this vital force. After obtaining it, it is imperative to retain possession, and this is precisely where your vision board serves its purpose. It facilitates the retention of the attained vibrations.

The magnitude of your vibrations and energy determine the trajectory of your life. One might possess minimal material wealth, yet exude the vibrancy and zest reminiscent of affluence and contentment. One can attain affluence while embodying the qualities of compassion and approachability. In order to attain your desired objectives in life, it is imperative to align your own vibrational frequency with that of the individual you aspire to be.

Eliminating Obstacles Hindering the Efficacy of Visualization

It will require a mere few moments to create mental images of your aspirations and ambitions. Throughout the course of the day, it remains imperative that one cultivates a favorable mindset, fostering the belief in their capacity to accomplish any objective they have determined to pursue. There are certain post-visualization practices that can mitigate the impact of the session on oneself. Should adequate caution not be exercised, there exists the possibility of regressing to one's original state, or, in a more dire scenario, forsaking one's aspirations and ambitions. The following delineates the obstacles that impede effective visualization and offers approaches to overcome them.

Entertaining negative thoughts. Negative thinking is occasionally misconstrued as being grounded in realism or pragmatism. Maintaining a positive outlook does not imply disregarding potential obstacles in addressing one's challenges. It unequivocally implies that you refuse to let these barriers impede your determination to actualize your aspirations and objectives. It is imperative that you acquire the ability to discern and identify these assertions internally as follows:

This is impossible.
My current financial resources are insufficient to cover the expenses associated with this.
I aspire to fulfill my aspirations, yet I must take into consideration the needs and well-being of my family.
I aspire to accomplish this, however, I find myself faced with [fill in the blanks].

Upon the realization of such thoughts, it is imperative to consciously affirm to oneself the decision to no longer indulge in or entertain these thoughts. Whenever you happen to encounter thoughts of them once more, promptly endeavor to suppress them.

Involving with negative people. There may exist individuals who have the potential to undermine and inadvertently deter your pursuit of goals and aspirations. Exercise caution around individuals who:" "Be wary of individuals who:" "Exercise vigilance regarding individuals who:" "Use caution when dealing with people who:" "Exercise prudence in relation to individuals who:" "Be on guard against individuals who:" "Take heed of individuals who:" "Exercise discretion with individuals who:" "Exercise circumspection when dealing with individuals who:

They harbored feelings of envy towards your accomplishments and intentionally sought to hinder your progress through disparagement.

Possessing good intentions and sincere motivations, they find themselves hindered by their habitually pessimistic mindset.

are attempting to conform you within their preconceived notion of success.

When engaging with individuals of such nature, one has the option to effectively communicate, with a firm yet assertive tone, their unwavering commitment towards pursuing their aspirations, or alternatively, to limit or altogether abstain from associating with said individuals. Do not permit these individuals to impede your pursuit of a more enriching existence.

Action Point:
What are the detrimental thought patterns that impede your cognitive alignment with your envisioned objective? Write them down.

_____
_____
_____
_____
_____
_____
_____
_____
_____

By what means do you attain these pessimistic thought patterns?

_____
_____

_____

_____

_____

_____

Are you acquainted with individuals in your sphere who detract from your pursuit of your aspirations? Who are they? What measures can be taken to safeguard one's determination in the pursuit of their goals and aspirations, ensuring they remain untouched by external influences?

_____

_____

_____

_____

_____

The recognition of these factors enhances one's level of consciousness. Upon acquiring an understanding of these obstacles, you will be equipped with the knowledge to mitigate their impact on your level of motivation. Once you have recognized these obstacles, proceed to affirm to yourself that you will not permit these barriers to dictate the course of your life.

The Essence of Excellence in Data Visualization Design

The field of data visualization involves the transformative power of adept design in converting extensive, intricate, and bewildering data into a captivating visual representation. Data not only transforms into fundamental information but also becomes comprehensible and effortlessly discernible. With such adeptness, your communication can reach a broad range of recipients. It is anticipated that one's design would effectively resonate with a diverse range of individuals, spanning from the highest level of organizational hierarchy to the average online user perusing content.

Given the repeated emphasis on the notion of a "good design," it prompts inquiry into the specific elements that define a design as good. Does this pertain to the methodology utilized in the creation of a visual design? Alternatively, what message does it convey? Alternatively, one could inquire about the extent to which the concept is positively received by the audience. Does it consist of a single option or is it a combination of the aforementioned choices? Regrettably, there is no definitive criterion for determining what constitutes a well-crafted visual. However, there are several approaches that can ensure that your design is unambiguous, comprehensive, and effectively communicates with your intended audience. These may include:

Creating visuals that are readily recognizable

Designing a simplified and uncluttered layout.

Arranging your content in a manner that facilitates easy comprehension for the viewer, requiring minimal exertion.

Achieving optimal impact through the strategic utilization of fonts, shapes, and colors.

By implementing elements of contrast, hierarchy, and balance, one can effectively direct the viewer's attention towards the most significant attributes.

As individuals, we often overlook the value of our senses. The act of perceiving, analyzing, and assimilating our surroundings using our visual, auditory, and tactile senses is inherent, often causing us to inadvertently overlook its significance. Therefore, we encounter over one hundred distinct visual stimuli on a daily basis, without sincerely devoting our attention to them. Visual perception is the cognitive capacity of the human brain to assimilate and interpret visual stimuli. Consequently, it is imperative that we acquire a comprehensive comprehension of the cognitive mechanisms involved in visual perception, enabling us to effectively and decisively make design choices for our own purposes.

The process of perception is a cognitive mechanism, with the eyes and the brain serving as essential entities in the realm of visual perception. The brain processes information that is gathered by the sensory organs. Conclusions are seldom derived solely from one's visual, auditory, olfactory, gustatory, or tactile senses. Conversely, this data is transmitted to the cerebral cortex for the purpose of being meticulously analyzed and subsequently comprehended. Comprehension of design elements and principles in visual perception is essential for the creation of a robust and highly impactful design.

Each design element plays a significant role in conveying messages to the intended audience, forming an integral part of a visual language. Furthermore, acquiring insight into the manner in which individuals perceive and analyze visual information will enhance the likelihood of creating a composition that audiences readily grasp and actively participate in. Let us now focus our attention on exploring our senses and cognitive science in order to gain a comprehensive understanding of the scientific principles that govern visual perception. By doing so, we will enhance our ability to discern and appreciate the intricacies of our designs.

Chapter Five: A Comprehensive Overview of Data Analysis

Having acquired a notion of the concept of data mining, it is now pertinent to delve into comprehending data analysis and the various procedures employed in data analysis, albeit in a succinct manner. We shall explore these concepts in greater depth as we progress further into the book.

Data analysis refers to the systematic procedure of transforming, purifying, and modeling collected information with the aim of uncovering concealed patterns and insights within the dataset, thus facilitating the acquisition of well-informed decisions. The objective of data analysis is to uncover valuable insights embedded within the dataset and make informed decisions based on the findings of the analysis.

Why Use Data Analysis?

If one desires to progress in one's personal or professional endeavors, it is imperative to engage in data analysis with regards to the information gathered. If your business fails to experience growth, it is imperative to reflect upon and acknowledge any potential errors committed, subsequently making efforts to rectify and overcome them. Furthermore, it is imperative to devise a strategy to mitigate the reoccurrence of such errors. In the event of business expansion, it is imperative to proactively consider implementing requisite modifications in processes to further enhance the business's growth trajectory. It is imperative that the information be examined in accordance with the business procedures and data.

Software for the Analysis of Data

One may utilize various data analysis tools to manipulate and process data. These tools facilitate the examination of correlations and associations among diverse sets of data, thereby increasing analytical ease. Furthermore, these tools facilitate the identification of latent insights or patterns within the dataset.

Data Analysis Types

The subsequent examples delineate various methodologies for data analysis.

Text Analysis

This particular mode of analysis is commonly referred to as data mining, a topic that has been extensively examined in the preceding chapters.

Statistical Analysis

By employing statistical analysis, it is possible to discern the occurrence of a certain event by evaluating historical data. This particular mode of analysis encompasses the subsequent series of procedures:

Collection

Processing of information

Analysis

Interpretation of the results

Delivery of the findings" "Conveyance of the outcomes" "Exposition of the data" "Communication of the conclusions" "Articulation of the findings

Data modeling

Employing statistical analysis facilitates the examination of sample data. "There exist two variations of statistical analysis:

Descriptive Analysis

In this analytical approach, one examines either the complete dataset or a subset of the condensed dataset represented by numerical values. This numerical data can be utilized to compute the measures of central tendency.

Inferential Analysis

Within this analytical investigation, a representative subset of the complete dataset is examined. One can opt for various samples and execute identical procedures to ascertain the composition of the dataset. This mode of analysis also provides insight into the organization of the dataset.

Diagnostic Analysis

Diagnostics analysis is employed to ascertain the causal factors leading to the occurrence of a specific event. This form of analysis harnesses statistical models to unveil any latent patterns and extract valuable insights from the given data set. One can utilize diagnostic analysis to ascertain any emerging issues in business processes and ascertain the underlying causes. Additionally, one can discern any analogous trends within the dataset in order to ascertain the possible existence of any comparable issues. This particular analytical approach empowers individuals to apply prescribed solutions to novel challenges.

Predictive Analysis

Predictive analysis involves the utilization of historical data to ascertain future occurrences. An illustrative instance is when you make a determination regarding the purchases you intend to engage in. Suppose you have an affinity for shopping and have recently purchased four dresses from your accumulated savings. Assuming that your salary were to increase twofold during the upcoming year, it is quite likely that you would be able to purchase a total of eight dresses. This serves as a simple illustration, but it is important to note that not all analyses will be as straightforward as this. You should take into consideration the various circumstances involved in conducting this analysis, given that the prices of clothing may fluctuate in the coming months.

Predictive analysis enables the derivation of future projections by analyzing relevant historical and contemporary data. It is vital to emphasize that the outcomes attained merely constitute prognostications. The effectiveness of the employed model hinges upon the available data and one's ability to delve into its depths.

Prescriptive Analysis

The prescriptive analysis process involves leveraging the knowledge and outcomes derived from past analyses to inform the course of action necessary for resolving a present decision or problem. The majority of businesses have now adopted a data-centric approach, employing this method of analysis due to their requirement for both descriptive and prescriptive analyses in order to enhance data performance. Data professionals utilize these technologies and tools for the purpose of examining the data at hand and extracting meaningful outcomes.

Data Analysis Process

The methodology employed for data analysis is entirely contingent upon the data collected and the analytical tools or methodologies utilized for the examination and investigation of said data. It is imperative that you identify patterns within the dataset. With reference to the data and information you gather, you can acquire the essential knowledge to procure the ultimate outcome or inference. The procedural steps that are carried out are:

Data Requirement Gathering

Data Collection

Data Cleaning

Data Analysis

Data Interpretation

Data Visualization

Data Acquisition Process

Regarding data analysis, it is imperative to ascertain the underlying purpose driving the necessity to undertake such an analysis. The goal of this particular phase is to ascertain the objective of your analysis. You are recommended to determine the specific form of analysis you wish to pursue, as well as the desired methodology to employ in conducting said analysis. In this stage, it is advised that you ascertain the parameters of your analysis, along with the methodologies and metrics that will be employed to gather and evaluate this data. It is crucial to ascertain the underlying reasons for the necessity of conducting an investigation, as well as to establish the specific methodologies that will be employed to execute this analysis.

Data Collection

Once the requirements are gathered, you will gain a comprehensive understanding of the available data and the metrics that need to be assessed. You will also gain insight into what to anticipate from your discoveries. Now is the appropriate moment for you to gather the necessary data that aligns with your business's specifications. Once the data has been gathered from the various sources, it is imperative that you undertake the necessary steps to process and meticulously arrange it prior to engaging in any analysis. Given that you acquire data from various sources, it is necessary to uphold a record that includes the date of acquisition and pertinent details pertaining to each source.

Data Cleaning

The data you gather might not be pertinent to your needs or may prove inconsequential for your analysis. Consequently, it is imperative that you cleanse it prior to undertaking these procedures. The data may contain extraneous spaces, inaccuracies, and redundant entries, necessitating the need for thorough cleansing and elimination of errors. It is imperative to undertake the task of data cleaning prior to analyzing the data, as the accuracy and reliability of your analytical outcomes directly hinge upon the quality of data cleansing.

Data Analysis
Through the systematic collection, processing, and refinement of data, one can derive meaningful insights through analysis. When engaging in data manipulation, it is necessary to devise a methodology for extracting pertinent information from the dataset. In the event that the required information is not located, it is imperative to acquire additional data from the dataset. In this particular stage of the procedure, you have the opportunity to utilize the tools, methodologies, and software designed for the purpose of analyzing data, thus allowing you to interpret, comprehend, scrutinize, and derive essential findings as per the stipulated specifications.

Data Interpretation

Once the data has been thoroughly analyzed, it is appropriate for you to proceed with the interpretation of the findings. Once you obtain the outcomes, you have the option of presenting the analysis through a chart or a table. The findings of the analysis can be utilized to determine the optimal course of action available to you.

Data Visualization

A significant proportion of individuals frequently employ data visualization, often in the form of graphical representations and charts. Put simply, when data is presented using a graphical representation, it facilitates comprehension and cognitive processing for the human mind. Data visualization is employed for the purpose of discerning latent information, patterns, and associations within the given dataset. By carefully analyzing the relationships or correlations among the data points, one can acquire significant and consequential insights.

Integrate your Meditation Practice with Creative Visualization

This chapter shall delve into the integration of the heightened concentration achieved through your meditation endeavors, effectively employing it in the realm of creative visualization. Enhance your meditation practice to a degree where it bestows great vitality upon the alternative reality that you are envisioning.

As previously stated in the preceding chapter, it is imperative to undertake this action in order to elicit a profound level of emotional involvement within oneself. Rest assured, irrespective of the multitude of intellectual debates engaged in or the abundance of information acquired, true authenticity can only be attained through genuine emotional connection.

Furthermore, it is evident that you possess a well-defined and explicit vision, which encompasses a logically coherent and plausible pathway towards attaining the desired ultimate success. However, it is crucial to emphasize that the emotional aspect of this vision holds utmost significance and cannot be overlooked, for it is this emotional connection that truly brings the vision to life and renders it meaningful. Visualization engenders the development of an emotional aspect.

Allow me to elaborate on the manner in which it accomplishes this. Initially, it is imperative to elaborate on the specifics while engaging in the process of visualization. This task is performed within a three-dimensional framework. You exhibit a comprehensive awareness beyond mere visual perception. Additionally, you envision sensory experiences such as olfactory, gustatory, tactile, and auditory perceptions, along with the corresponding emotional response, that would be elicited in the event of your existence within that alternate realm. It encompasses more than meets the eye. It extends beyond the visual elements. It is imperative that the experience incorporates olfactory, auditory, tactile, and gustatory sensations. Put simply, it must strive to attain the highest level of realism.

Why do this?

What is the rationale behind requiring a substantial level of realism during the process of visualization? Initially, one cultivates a perception of urgency. When one engages in the act of visualization with a lesser degree of clarity, it becomes readily apparent to the mind that one is merely conceptualizing an alternative version of reality. It's still not real. It remains disengaged from the present reality of your existence. Ultimately, it's still theoretical. Once your cognition processes this information, employing defensive mechanisms becomes quite effortless.

We are all beings who seek comfort. Our perpetual inclination is to opt for the course of minimal opposition. Your cognitive faculties are disinclined to endeavor towards the requisite effort necessary for its realization, resulting in its casual dismissal as a pleasant abstraction or future conjecture unrelated to your current state of affairs.

Alternatively, when adopting a 3-dimensional visualization approach and immersing oneself in the emotional aspects of the vision, a profound sense of urgency and relevance is cultivated. Your sense of conviction is activated, prompting you to acknowledge the vividness of this possibility. Through repeated affirmations, the phrase "this can happen" evolves into "this will happen."

The secret? Immediacy. The greater the degree of immediacy or impending nature of the emotion, the more probable it becomes that your brain will interpret that visualization as an envisioned outcome rather than a mere possibility, particularly as you intensify your concentration upon it.

Another advantage that is obtained is the increased degree of emotional urgency. It is imperative to bear in mind that experiences lack authenticity unless one perceives them through their emotions. Without experiencing the fear, the thrill, and the profound sense of determined pursuit, even the most meticulously crafted strategies will yield limited results, as they are merely objective information and quantitative figures. They\\\'re just logistics. It is crucial for you to cultivate an innate and discernible sense of urgency, as it will serve as a driving force to consistently propel you into action on a daily basis.

Not only do you persist in contemplating your vision, but you also articulate it, experience the intricacies of emotional exhilaration, and take concrete actions towards its realization. This marks the point of transformation in one's life, wherein one's actions and demeanor undergo a significant shift as a direct consequence of the unwavering focus on a particular vision. Consequently, it leads me to present the ultimate advantage that arises from the practice of 3D visualization - emotional commitment.

You begin viewing your vision as an inherent component of your personal identity. It is now intrinsically entwined with your experience. It is no longer a creation of your intellect. On the contrary, it constitutes an integral aspect of your identity. If one is capable of attaining this, relinquishing it becomes exceedingly arduous. You will persistently scrutinize that perception until a transformation occurs within your mindset, consequently influencing your emotional states and behavioral patterns.

Strengthen the integration process with confirmations

After successfully cultivating your meditation-induced concentration on your visual perception to foster a keen sense of urgency, emotional intensity, and profound emotional commitment, the subsequent stage involves solidifying this integration process. In essence, you desire to establish a state of permanence to the greatest extent possible.

May I inquire about the methodology to accomplish this task? Turn to affirmations. You consistently reiterate assertions that manifest your envisioned outcome. Once more, it is important to note that there is no definitive correct or incorrect response in this situation, as I am not aware of the details regarding your vision. Consequently, it is necessary for you to transcribe a precise affirmation that aligns with your vision.

As an illustration, envisioning a future where you reside in a lavish residence worth $6 million nestled within the picturesque California hills, you can manifest this desired outcome by articulating affirmations such as, "I am prepared to manifest this aspiration through diligent commitment to the development of my comprehensive business plan on a daily basis." I am prepared to acquire this house as I engage in daily activities to establish connections and cultivate professional relationships.

Your assertion should fulfill the following three criteria. In the first place, it is imperative to assert your preparedness. Furthermore, it must validate your deservingness. It is essential to ensure that you acknowledge and assert your worthiness and deservingness of that vision. It is advisable to avoid finding oneself in a circumstance where personal doubts of being fraudulent or an impostor persist in one's mind. That approach is not viable. You are engaging in self-sabotage through your actions.

Your assertions should not exclusively center on your state of preparedness. Signifying your inclination to proactively pursue the realization of your aspirations in the present moment, as well as your deservingness. It is imperative that you possess a sense of worthiness towards your aspirations.

Ultimately, it is necessary for you to acknowledge and assert your inherent competencies. If not already possessed, one would acquire the requisite skills and talents essential for realizing their dreams. Do not underestimate the significance of it; your assertions serve as the fundamental building blocks for fostering imaginative visualization.

Merely engaging in creative visualization is insufficient. It is imperative to provide solid corroborative evidence as affirmations carry significant weight in materializing one's intentions.

Your unconscious mind registers and takes note of the verbal expressions you employ. As one replaces negative self-talk with positive affirmations, the subconscious mind becomes receptive to these thoughts and strives to manifest them in reality. While your prior level of confidence may have been lacking, consistently affirming that I possess confidence and actively engaging in risk-taking will undoubtedly foster an increase in my self-assurance. Commence the process of translating your vision into tangible reality by utilizing affirmations. There is no more opportune moment than the present.

Chapter Three - Contemplation and Imagery

Prior to merging the two forces of meditation and visualization, it is imperative to have diligently honed skills in both practices. If you are unfamiliar with the practice of meditation, it is important to note that meditation offers various advantages, including the restoration of energy levels and the facilitation of focused and calm mental states. Hence, it becomes apparent that a correlation exists between meditation and visualization, as both enable concentration - one on inner serenity and the other on identifying the elements necessary to foster a sense of contentment in one's life.

Meditation

Assume a relaxed posture. There is no necessity for employing intricate leg positioning during this type of meditative practice. You must be comfortable. Upon observing the positioning of this lady's head, one can discern its optimal alignment for the purpose of inhaling revitalizing air. If it entails occupying a spot on the beach of your preference or adjacent to your personal swimming pool, such locations may indeed suffice; however, it is noteworthy that this can also be accomplished within the confines of an indoor setting. Ensure that your attire does not impose limitations and that you attain a state of complete comfort prior to commencing the breathing exercises.

In a formal tone, you can express the same idea as follows: "It is recommended that you inhale through your nasal passages, retain the breath within your abdomen, and subsequently exhale from the diaphragm for a duration slightly exceeding your exhalation."

Consider it from this perspective:

1. Inhale deeply, perceiving the ingress of air into your being and directing your complete focus towards it – Tally 8.

2. Maintain the air - Enumeration 6.

3. Exhale using the diaphragm – Proceed to 10

Engage in repetitive cycles of inhalation through the nasal passages and exhalation through the oral cavity, while maintaining a heightened awareness of the airflow traversing your body. Redirect your attention away from anything that causes you distress. Your utmost focus during this course of action ought to center on the regulation of your respiration.

After successfully attaining the aptitude to focus entirely on your respiration, proceed to engage in this practice for approximately 10 minutes. This improves cognitive acuity and enhances the ability to concentrate effectively. The oxygen circulating within your body will contribute to promoting a state of calmness.

Visualization

Maintain your current position, however, on this occasion, as you inhale, concentrate your thoughts on the object or concept you wish to visualize. This sentiment has the potential to evoke a profound sense of tranquility. It could encompass the sensation of monetary gain or accomplishment, or it could pertain to any aspiration that resonates deeply within one's innermost desires.

While inhaling, utter phrases that strengthen the imagery you conjure. For instance:

"I feel great energy."

"I feel great wealth."

As you release your breath, you experience the effortless transfer of that vitality emanating from within you, permeating the external realm, only to be reintegrated upon the subsequent inhalation.

Continuously fostering such visualization and bearing in mind that its integration into your daily routine is imperative for the realization of desired outcomes. Although it may have required me nearly 50 years to achieve a proficient level in playing the piano, I successfully accomplished this by consistently reinforcing the concept. I could have allowed the pressing worldly matters in my life to take precedence and relinquished my pursuit of the dream. If I had undertaken such an action, it is plausible that I would have never acquired the skill of playing the piano. Nevertheless, the intensity of my dream or mental imagery was so profound that it assimilated into my very essence, as should your aspirations.

It is imperative to integrate both meditation and visualization into your daily routine to ensure the manifestation and fulfillment of your visualizations. Do not entertain aspirations for unattainable physical feats, for they shall remain beyond reach. If you possess straight hair and desire to achieve curls, it is necessary to curl your hair. Physical appearance is not the determining factor. It pertains to one's emotional state and accomplishments in life. If your desire is to enhance your perceived beauty, it is indeed advisable to engage in the practice of envisioning yourself as a person possessing exceptional aesthetic qualities. Such visualization will effectively cultivate a compelling aura befitting the concept of beauty.

Carefully observe someone who catches your attention due to their beauty. Upon initial observation, one's immediate perception indicates that the individual possesses exceptional physical attractiveness. That individual likely possesses remarkable charisma, which constitutes a distinct and separate quality. The potential misalignment of her nose or the slightly smaller size of her eyes hold no significance. She exudes an aesthetic allure that is a reflection of her internal beauty. Hence, anyone can attain that sentiment and is capable of emanating it towards others merely by having faith in their own ability to embody what they aspire to become.

Visualization Techniques

Utilizing visualization techniques activates the latent potential of our minds, enabling us to triumph and attain our objectives. Visualization entails the cognitive practice of employing mental imagery to vividly depict ourselves engaging in desired experiences. The power of our imagination outweighs all other factors as it is the sole requisite for the entire process. Undoubtedly, imagination surpasses knowledge.

Knowledge has limits. Imagination is limitless. The faculty of imagination empowers us to craft the existence we aspire to lead, alongside all other accompanying experiences. It elevates our emotional well-being as we contemplate our aspirations, engendering positive sentiments within us. It was beyond our knowledge that our unassuming imaginations held the key to resolving all our difficulties and scaling the pinnacle of achievement. With this newfound understanding that imagination knows no bounds, to what extent do you believe you can truly excel?

Elite athletes employ visualization strategies to achieve prowess in their respective athletic disciplines. A scientifically conducted study involving four groups of athletes has provided evidence to support the notion that individuals possessing exceptional visualization abilities have a higher likelihood of attaining victory compared to those who solely rely on physical training. It can be convincingly inferred that the events stored in our subconscious bear an undeniable resemblance to the objective reality witnessed in the external world.

Treasure Draw

The term "treasure drawing" refers to the process of creating a visual representation of an object or concept that holds significant value or interest to us. We typically opt to depict it, provided that it is feasible to do so. We strategically position it in convenient locations for daily visibility, such as on the kitchen wall, the bedroom ceiling, or the fridge door. The act of engaging in treasure drawing yields a distinct depiction of your genuine aspirations, thereby facilitating the manifestation of your objectives.

Reformed Memory Visualization

The process of employing reformed memory visualization is utilized as a means of reconciling conflicts and relinquishing former resentments. By employing this methodology, individuals engage in the process of envisioning mental representations that tactically substitute negative elements with positive counterparts, particularly by infusing them with the desired emotion. Fundamentally, it modifies the unfavorable past in order to generate a favorable future. This offers significant support to individuals who have undergone a negative experience in their past. As an example, instead of indulging in grief over tragedies or assigning blame, you have a tendency to channel those emotions towards personal growth, believing that they have a profound impact on your life. After retrieving the memory of the incident, it is important to endeavor to maintain composure and serenity by adopting a tranquil breathing technique, while avoiding any emergence of anger. It will require a significant investment of time to repeatedly reproduce identical scenes, but with persistence, you will eventually achieve your goal.

Open Visualization

The process of engaging in the open visualization technique can be described as mentally creating and directing a movie, allowing the individual to exert full control over the unfolding narrative. A austere and contemplative environment is beneficial for an activity in which a student can mentally perceive the perspective of a distinct visual encounter. Engaging in this activity is most effectively enhanced by the presence of music.

Directed Visualization

Directed visualization is commonly defined as the technique wherein one selects and immerses oneself in a mental representation of a specific setting, subsequently experiencing it with utmost realism. Individuals employ this method of visualization to identify an internal locus wherein a profound connection to their intuition resides. Individuals who employ this particular form of visualization effectively generate solutions by employing the mental images they have envisaged. Through the act of forming mental images, their consciousness prompts the emergence of both inquiries and responses.

Examples

Visualization can serve as a valuable tool to guide an individual who is facing uncertainty towards the correct path. You have the opportunity to engage in visualization seminars, during which you will have the privilege of listening to a knowledgeable speaker who can guide you in maximizing your potential through visualization, in addition to the immense assistance this book has already rendered. Moreover, orators possess the ability to raise your enthusiasm levels through their eloquent and lively speeches. Furthermore, one-on-one sessions are offered to individuals seeking a more tailored and intimate approach to honing their visualization techniques. Engaging in a one-on-one session can also cater to your individual requirements. Engaging in this introspective exploration has also been found to be beneficial for one's overall well-being. In due course, you will experience an improvement in your well-being and a discernible emergence of favorable transformations. Acquiring knowledge through the utilization of visualization techniques will serve as a catalyst in rejuvenating both your mental and emotional faculties, thereby facilitating the process of manifesting your desired outcomes. By exercising steadfast self-discipline and relying on astute intuition, you position yourself on a trajectory to attain the rewards commensurate with your efforts.

To maximize the benefits derived from treasure draw, one can undertake additional measures to enhance the power of visualization, beyond merely specifying objectives and the corresponding milestones throughout the journey. Please be advised that you are not strictly compelled to depict the exact items you desire. Furthermore, it is possible to extract images from magazines, be it an aesthetically pleasing dwelling, a pristine automobile, or any visual representation that embodies one's desires. In the event that magazines are unavailable, it is possible to retrieve images from the Internet and subsequently produce printouts. The subsequent task you are required to perform involves affixing them onto a visualization board. This object is merely a plain cardboard box or an illustration board that has been adorned with a collage encompassing all the elements you desire. The final action entails affixing it to the wall in a location that facilitates daily visibility.

Please be advised that visualization and imagination share a fundamental similarity in their approach. To conceptualize something is to merely envision it. The human intellect is of such great splendor that it possesses the capacity to perceive and comprehend data conveyed by an image, alongside its cognitive functioning. The subconscious mind elicits an autonomous behavioral and emotional reaction in response to each visual stimulus it encounters. Initially, one may experience limitations in one's ability to create vivid mental imagery; however, through consistent dedication and perseverance, significant improvement can be achieved. It is not required to possess expertise in the art of visualization; however, it is necessary to possess an adequate level of proficiency independently.

Every individual possesses aspirations in life that they aim to achieve. Whether you are an athlete striving to enhance your performance, an artist endeavoring to cultivate greater creativity, or an individual aspiring to advance their career and explore diverse avenues of success. Creative visualization is a powerful technique that can effectively facilitate the expansion of one's consciousness and enable the attainment of desired objectives with remarkable ease.

The competency of imaginative visualization stimulates the right hemisphere of your brain and triggers the activity of your prefrontal cortex. It facilitates the enhancement of your creative aptitude while enabling novel perspectives and insights. As you cultivate your faculties of imagination, you will progressively refine your aptitude for visualization. Consequently, as you dedicate effort towards honing your capacity for visualization, you will swiftly realize an augmentation in the quality and abundance of your imaginative ideas. The amalgamation of these elements contributes to the fortification of your mental capacities.

This is an acquired proficiency that individuals can master by employing meditation methodologies and harnessing their creative faculties, thereby broadening their cognitive horizons and effectively manifesting accomplishments that may appear arduous or unattainable. Although it is possible to utilize creative visualization techniques independently of meditation, integrating all aspects of these cognitive training methods will enable you to swiftly attain peak proficiency and achieve a significantly heightened rate of success. Furthermore, as one becomes more proficient in the practice of creative visualization, their capacity for imagination will concurrently intensify. This heightened imaginative prowess will consequently foster enhanced aptitude in resolving daily challenges.

This book will impart all the necessary knowledge and techniques required to master the art of meditation and effectively transform it into enhanced creative visualization practices. It will also elucidate certain effective techniques for fostering imaginative thinking and enhancing cognitive receptivity to both the physical realm and the seemingly intangible metaphysical dimension. You will soon be making significant progress towards the fulfillment of all your aspirations!

Crucial Considerations to Bear in Mind

Persevere, despite any delays that may hinder your progress towards achieving your desired destination. Persevere in honing your skills and in due course, myriad possibilities shall unfold before you.

Creative visualization involves transforming your cognitive perspective of the surrounding environment, facilitating the attraction of favorable energies towards oneself. It aids in the cultivation of a receptive mindset towards the desired achievements, as well as in fostering the exploration of novel prospects capable of guiding you towards your intended destination.

By harnessing the power of your imagination, your newfound proficiency in meditation, and the abundance of positive energy within you, you possess the ability to effortlessly materialize the deserving aspects of your life. Enjoy your new life!

The Impact of Creative Visualization

The utilization of Creative Visualization expedites the process of therapeutic recovery.

Creative visualization is frequently employed by athletes to enhance their performance. A golfer is reputed for mentally envisaging an impeccable swing on multiple occasions. This will enhance the cognitive activation of muscle memory.

Now, let us examine a widely recognized study that explores the impact of creative visualization on athletic performance.

A grouping methodology was employed to divide the contingent of Olympic athletes into three distinct cohorts. Group 1 was provided with comprehensive physical training. The athletes comprising Group 2 underwent a physical training regimen constituting

75% of their overall program, with the remaining 25% encompassing mental conditioning. On the contrary, athletes belonging to Group 3 were subjected to a balanced combination of both physical training and mental conditioning, with equal emphasis placed on each aspect, totaling 50% for each category. It was observed that the athletes belonging to Group 3 demonstrated the most outstanding performance. Therefore, this finding allows us to infer that mental imagery serves as a catalyst for motor responses, a principle that is broadly acknowledged within the domains of sports psychology and neuroscience.

Creative Visualization accelerates the process of healing.

We have encountered numerous instances of the efficacious impact of creative visualization on the facilitation of the healing process. Individuals have been recognized for providing accounts of personal recovery, including cancer remission, and various other health conditions through the utilization of creative imagery. A man in his eighties was able to vividly perceive the imagery of blood emanating from his veins, with avian creatures partaking in the consumption of the toxins released by the ailing cells. Frankly speaking, it is crucial to have faith in oneself, as this belief will facilitate the natural progression of events.

Chapter Seven: Overcoming Restrictive Thought Patterns

The utilization of imaginative introspection has the potential to significantly facilitate the attainment of remarkable accomplishments in one's personal and professional endeavors. However, there exists individuals for whom specific aspects remain resistant to change, either due to the challenging nature of the transformation or the current limitations of our circumstances. The potency of creative visualization is substantial; nevertheless, it does possess certain constraints. These limitations are inherent within ourselves, rather than residing in the realm of power.

Frequently, we confine ourselves and are unable to envision beyond a specific circumference. We confine our contemplations and embrace a limited scope of beliefs, thereby constricting ourselves within the realm of our actual lived experiences.

It is imperative to maintain an open-minded perspective and strive for ambitious goals. This will bring us closer to broader prospects or potential. The constraints lie within the confines of our own thoughts, and it is incumbent upon us to instigate a transformation. The implementation of the change may require a period of time for realization. Minor and transient fluctuations may transpire expeditiously, however, substantial metamorphoses will indubitably necessitate a more protracted duration.

It is essential to maintain unwavering belief and persevere in one's efforts. The outcomes will commence manifesting automatically.

Chapter Six: The Power of Purposeful Effort

The concluding stage of the creative visualization process involves embracing proactive measures. When the universe provides an occurrence of opportunity, it is imperative to seize it.

As an instance, an aspiration of yours is to pursue a postgraduate degree in a foreign country. If you have diligently engaged in daily visualization practices, you can anticipate forthcoming opportunities that may materialize, such as the potential acquisition of a scholarship for international study or the prospect of participating in a professional development program sponsored by your current employer. It is imperative to acknowledge and seize these opportunities.

If you aspire to visit Greece or France, commence contacting reputable travel agents and diligently search for reasonably priced airfare and lodging options. To enhance your earnings, focus on refining your skills in order to attain a promotion. If you aspire to initiate a business venture, approach a venture capitalist and explore the potential of securing investment for your entrepreneurial endeavor.

Visualizing programs the mind to initiate action. It presents opportunities, individuals, and circumstances along your path that can facilitate the realization of your aspirations. It is incumbent upon you to seize those opportunities and make earnest efforts to materialize your aspirations.

If pursuing a career as a lawyer is your aspiration, it is imperative that you enroll in a reputable law school. If one aspires to a career as a pilot, it is essential to undergo the requisite training.

It is important to bear in mind that the effective implementation of visualization and affirmation practices hinges on the simultaneous undertaking of requisite actions to materialize our aspirations.

Chapter 4: The Phenomenon of Materialization

Before you start the manifestation process, I recommend you have a clear vision of your desired outcome.

If your objective entails embarking on a journey from New York to Hollywood, it would be prudent to devise a thorough navigational itinerary that encompasses the entire route leading to Tinsel Town. In the absence of a map or GPS for navigation assistance, one might find oneself anywhere in the vicinity stretching from Seattle down to the Mexican border.

Similarly, it is imperative that you commence with a thorough comprehension of your genuine aspirations in the process of manifestation. I have had the opportunity to collaborate with numerous clients who expressed their desire to attract greater wealth. Upon closer examination, however, these individuals ultimately came to the realization that their true desires were centered around acquiring a home, settling their student loans, or nurturing a sense of financial stability. Articulate and elucidate your intention with precision.

There is nothing wrong with having a prosperity mindset. Ultimately, abundance is inherently granted to you by virtue of your existence. Being precise enhances the process of materialization and brings about the manifestation of your exact desire in the tangible realm.

I have observed that a significant number of individuals struggle with the process of manifestation due to a lack of comprehension regarding the inherent significance of the present moment. They lead their existence trapped in an unceasing cycle of reminiscing about bygone moments, reminiscing about former partners, ruminating over past errors, or fixating excessively on the future, consumed by apprehensions of potential eventualities. Through our current state of awareness, we exert an influence on the course of future events. Our future is impacted by our present actions.

By directing our attention to the present moment, we bring forth the realization of our aspirations. By harmonizing our awareness with our aspirations, we effectively materialize our aspirations.

The Energy of Alignment

In order to materialize a significant financial return of one million dollars, it is essential to harmonize oneself with the concepts of abundance, affluence, and prosperity.

Let us consider the individual residing in the vicinity, who has obtained a triumphant lottery ticket. It is possible that you are acquainted with his background. He resided in a trailer that lacked heating or air conditioning within the confines of his residence. Based on his attire, one would not have surmised that he possessed considerable wealth. Nevertheless, inwardly, he had associated himself with a million-dollar lottery victory. In addition to perceiving himself as a recipient of a lottery prize, he possessed the ability to manifest his desires to the Universe. The Universe, in a synchronized fashion, acted in response to this energy and ensured his alignment with the opportunity to purchase a ticket that would yield success.

He refrained from delineating the specific steps he would take to manifest his aspiration; rather, he engaged in the mental exercise of envisioning triumph and internalizing a victorious result. Regardless of his awareness, he was flawlessly adhering to the process of manifestation.

1. Energy Alignment.
2. Enriching visualizations with profound emotional intensity.
3. A disposition characterized by appreciation and felicity.
4. Release to the Universe.

A significant number of individuals are unable to bring forth their desired outcomes due to self-imposed obstacles. Let us examine the process of manifestation and discern areas of success and failure, respectively.

1. Energy Alignment. We perceive ourselves as undeserving of embracing our aspirations. We are excessively preoccupied with the notion of scarcity, disregarding our true potential to attain a million dollars.

2. Emotion-laden visualization was not employed; our desire lacked any semblance of joy, and we harbored no conviction in our ability to attain victory. Our dream remained devoid of any divine spark. We failed to witness the act of grasping the triumphant ticket, along with the subsequent elation that ensued upon realizing our victory.

3. We exhibited a deficiency in expressing gratitude for our possessions and a lack of acknowledgment for our blessings. We were of the opinion that others were more worthy of attaining such a victory, whereas we did not consider ourselves to be deserving of such an outcome.

4. By neglecting to surrender to a higher power, or the cosmic force governing our existence, we did not relinquish our convictions. Instead, we allowed ourselves to wallow in a form of self-indulgent sorrow, clutching onto our sense of victimhood without ever embracing the essence of love, joy, and peace, nor acknowledging that we emerged triumphant.

On one occasion, while I was engaged in the pursuit of materializing the prospect of having a child, I came across the most exquisite carousel displayed in a boutique window. The cost totaled

$25.00, a sum I initially considered an indulgent outlay, yet I found it highly enticing. I envisioned it occupying a prominent place within the bedroom of my prospective offspring.

The scorching heat characteristic of July in Florida enveloped the region, making it feel unbearably hot, the kind of heat one can only experience in Florida. Upon my arrival at home, my mind became occupied with thoughts of the carrousel, eventually leading me into a state of slumber, where I indulged in pleasant fantasies of the carrousel adorning the nursery of my forthcoming offspring. Shortly thereafter, I awoken to the sound of the telephone's incessant ringing.

During the winter season when we were in the process of clearing our land, we took the initiative to place an advertisement in the local newspaper, offering the opportunity to purchase a pick-up load of wood for the price of $25.00. As previously mentioned, we had now reached the midpoint of summer and the brief three-line advertisement had already passed by. My spouse and I inadvertently overlooked it.

On that midsummer day, my slumber was interrupted by the ceaseless ringing of the telephone. A gentleman on the opposite end of the telephone inquired as to whether we still possess wood available for purchase. Due to the surplus, he arrived and collected a significant quantity of firewood, for which he willingly offered payment of $25.00, coincidentally corresponding with the precise cost of the carrousel.

Despite the physicians' prognosis, I indeed succeeded in bringing forth a son, albeit without acquiring the carrousel. Nonetheless, the instruction in manifestation remained ingrained in my memory.

Upon reclining for a brief slumber on that particular day, I failed to conceive any notion pertaining to the acquisition of an additional $25. I merely conceptualized the anticipated result. The sense of delight that enveloped me upon envisioning the exquisite appearance of the carousel within the nursery induced a serene slumber. I did not impose any limitations on the manner in which the sum of $25 would be obtained. I merely observed the carousel positioned on a tabletop. I began with the solution, and experienced a tranquil sense of contentment upon discovering it within the confines of my son's chamber. I disclosed the images to the Universe, whereby the Universe commenced the process of manifesting my aspiration.

Later that day, in the other part of the town, the elderly gentleman who had delivered the firewood discovered the local publication amidst a collection of outdated periodicals that he intended to discard. Our advertisement caught his attention. Despite the fact that it was during the height of summer, he felt compelled to contact us. It remains both awe-inspiring and astonishing to witness the unfolding of events, yet this precisely illustrates the principles of manifestation. I had harmonized my awareness with the desired outcome, and through its unfathomable workings, the Universe manifested the necessary financial resources to materialize it.

When we establish alignment with our aspirations, infuse our energy with ardor, and express gratitude before surrendering it to the Universe, we receive the support of the cosmic realm and the divine. The manifestation of our desires shall be brought forth into the realm of reality by the forces of the Universe.

Should you harbor a sense of inadequacy towards your desires, the cosmos shall fortify such belief. The Universe possesses an inherent objectivity and will duly manifest in your reality whatever you contemplate and concentrate upon. It neither bestows rewards nor inflicts punishment. It will provide you with what you intentionally synchronize your thoughts, words, and emotions with. The actions you put forth are returned in manifold.

Rest assured, it is an unequivocal fact that God will never bestow upon you a dream without simultaneously providing the corresponding answer or solution. The divine force, inherent in the vast expanse of the cosmos, collaborates with you as a co-originator of your personal reality.

If one aspires to possess a residential dwelling, one must associate oneself with the concept of owning a home and thus, one's dwelling shall materialize in precise accordance with the perceived value and alignment that one deems oneself deserving of. If one is unable to wholeheartedly embrace the idea of residing in a pleasant suburban residence or a seaside condominium, the realization of such a desire will be elusive. Prior to inflating a bicycle tire, it is imperative to manually draw air into the hand pump, ensuring its readiness before initiating the tire-inflation process. The same principle applies when extracting water from a well. Prior to extracting well-water, it is necessary to initiate the pumping mechanism. It holds true for energy as well.

Harness the profound vitality residing within you and channel it into a state of unwavering fervor, where the pure exhilaration of materializing your aspiration takes shape. Induce a state of euphoria within yourself by fully embracing the delight of attaining what you yearn for. This phenomenon exemplifies the extraordinary power of human emotions. Your internal vitality serves as the driving force that materializes your aspirations within the realm of reality.

If one desires to acquire a car or a residence, when one permits the joy to emerge within, the sensation of possessing said car or traversing through the newfound abode. The immense vitality residing within you is the celestial flame that sparks the process of materialization within your being.

If you are seeking companionship, cultivate an abundance of love within yourself. Permit the profound emotional intensity of love to effervesce from within oneself until the depths of one's heart seem poised to explode from sheer elation. Immerse yourself in the profound emotional essence of love, and the immense forces of the Universe shall orchestrate extraordinary measures to manifest your deepest desires.

Allow us to engage in a guided process wherein we visualize the creation of a diamond necklace. Initially, it is necessary to abandon any pessimistic mindset, exemplified by thoughts like never being able to possess an item of such elegance or lacking the financial means to afford such opulence.

Kindly be aware, and I sincerely emphasize, that I categorically do not authorize the utilization of your credit card for the purchase of this necklace, as it will undoubtedly result in remorse and anxiety. This exercise is solely achievable through the process of manifestation.

Therefore, in this particular instance, let us position ourselves in accordance with the necklace. Commence with the solution, just as I initiated my small carousel.

State your intention. I hereby demonstrate the physical presence of a diamond necklace.

Envision the visual impact it would have when adorning your person. What will be the sensation of wearing it? Does it carry a substantial or minimal weight? Observe the radiant shimmer adorning your neckline. Could you please provide some insight into whether you perceive a smooth texture or if you are cognizant of the clearly defined edges? Consider the scenario in which acquaintances and unfamiliar individuals admire the visual appeal of the garment on your person. Visualize yourself gracefully acknowledging their compliments. Exert maximum effort to infuse this visualization with intense emotion and vivid imagery.

Conclude your visualization practice with a demeanor of appreciation. I express my gratitude to the divine entity, Father-Mother-God, for bestowing upon me this exquisite necklace. This manifestation or a superior outcome is currently evident in my existence. Subsequently, relinquish your mental image to the Universe with confidence, being assured that the Universe will actualize the acquisition of that necklace. After concluding this matter, release your attachment and acknowledge that you have successfully channeled your intentions towards manifesting a diamond necklace.

This exercise focused on a necklace, however, it possesses the potential to encompass any object of desire that an individual wishes to bring into reality.

The cosmos does not possess a concept of magnitude. It possesses knowledge solely of what exists. The Universe will effectively materialize the desired outcomes that you intend to collaboratively bring into existence. One can effortlessly construct a residence, find a companion, amass wealth in one's accounts, or, as I personally achieved, bring forth a delightful offspring.

Harmonize your consciousness and subconsciousness with your emotional essence, establishing a profound connection with your aspirations.

The final stage of the manifestation process involves the act of relinquishment. Release your grip and allow the Universe to effortlessly manifest your desires from the intangible realm into the tangible world.

Maintain a consistent state of positive contemplation regarding your desires throughout the entirety of your day, directing your energy towards a favorable outcome and possessing unwavering conviction that it shall manifest in your reality. Convey your thoughts assertively.

Your state of eternal bliss is presently at hand, provided you comprehend its veracity.

Now, let us turn our attention to the remarkable potency found within the declarative phrase "I am." Although previously alluded to, it is my intention to explore further the inherent strength encapsulated within these words, "I am."

Important Visualization Elements

Visualization is a method by which individuals harness the power of their imagination to attain desired outcomes aligned with their aspirations. You can harness the benefits of your innate imaginative capabilities. It constitutes the capacity to generate a cognitive representation, emotional perception, and conceptual thoughts. One can envision an imaginative representation of their emotions. Your objectives may encompass spiritual, intellectual, emotional, and physical aspects across varying levels. In order to employ this visualization effectively, it is imperative to hold firm conviction in your spiritual or metaphysical beliefs, while remaining open-minded to different notions.

Fundamental Guidelines for Optimal Visualization

Prior to engaging in the practice of visualization, it is imperative to acquire a comprehensive understanding of its fundamental principles. "Outlined below are several prescribed procedures that must be adhered to in order to achieve optimal visualization:

Set Personalized Goals

You are tasked with making a decision regarding something that you may find desirable to possess, comprehend, generate, or strive for. It could manifest in various aspects, encompassing alterations in one's character, interpersonal connections, professional circumstances, living situation, psychological well-being, enhanced financial status, aesthetics, physical well-being, and the resolution of communal or familial issues, among others. In the initial stage, it is necessary to carefully determine your aspirations that can be feasibly achieved in the foreseeable future. It is imperative to establish certain objectives that are devoid of significant opposition. One can enhance their positive emotions by acquiring the skill of visualization. Through consistent practice, one will acquire the skills to effectively handle complex and arduous matters.

Generate a Lucid Depiction or Concept

It is imperative to cultivate a distinct mental image, emotional response, or conceptual understanding in relation to a given situation or object. One may consider the matter from the perspective of the present tense and envision the desired scenario. Please endeavor to incorporate a multitude of details in order to enhance your level of concentration.

Direct your attention towards your objective

It is advisable to engage in a period of calm and contemplative meditation, wherein you are encouraged to summon and foster a particular mental image or concept. You may contemplate this matter during your designated period of meditation and incorporate it as a vital component of your existence. Maintain a composed and effortless attitude while directing your attention towards the objective. It is imperative to abstain from perceiving oneself as exerting excessive effort or expending an additional level of energy towards the achievement of a goal. It can impede your objectives rather than facilitating them.

Increase Positive Energy

Whilst directing your attention towards your specific objectives, it would be prudent to contemplate them from a constructive and uplifting standpoint. Assert firmly and definitively its existence, its imminent arrival, or its approach towards you. Envision yourself attaining or acquiring it. These assertions are commonly referred to as affirmations. When utilizing your affirmations, endeavor to temporarily set aside any disbelief or doubts. The attainment of the desired positive emotions through deliberate practice is increasingly becoming feasible and tangible.

Persist in following this process until you attain all of your individual objectives. Please be aware that you have the flexibility to modify your goals based on your individual requirements.

It constitutes a significant aspect of the process of human development and transformation. It is unnecessary to expend prolonged effort towards a goal, as there is a risk of losing interest. Once interest has been lost, it becomes necessary to revise one's current objectives. Take note of any alteration in your objectives. Obtain a clear state of mind in which your attention is not directed towards your previously established objectives. Please ensure to conclude the previous cycle and commence a fresh cycle. It will prevent instances of perplexity and heighten the sense of achievement.

Upon reaching the desired objective, it is imperative to deliberately recognize and acknowledge its successful achievement. You have the potential to attain the objects of your vision or desired outcomes. Upon attaining your objectives, it is imperative to demonstrate self-appreciation and express gratitude to the cosmos for its benevolence.

MINDFULNESS MEDITATION

FOR THE PURPOSE OF THE NARRATOR:
This meditation is straightforward,
however, longer pauses are necessary to
be observed between each sentence.
Kindly maintain a 30-second interval
between each line, unless specified
otherwise.

Prior to commencing today's exercise, I
kindly request that you locate a position
of comfort within a serene environment.
Please power down all electronic devices
and ensure that you are not interrupted.
It is imperative that you have
uninterrupted solitude for a minimum of
half an hour during this activity.
At your convenience, please proceed to
take three deep breaths, ensuring that
you inhale through your nasal passages
and exhale with controlled slowness
through your oral cavity.
Please, gently shut your eyes and make
an effort to clear your thoughts.
Take cognizance of each of your
thoughts, and subsequently relinquish

them, individually, as though they were merely ephemeral clouds on your periphery.

Breathe in at your customary speed via your nasal passage, maintain your breath for a span of four counts, and subsequently exhale gradually via your oral cavity.

Continue practicing until it becomes an innate habit: breathe in, retain, and gradually release. Kindly articulate your statement at a slower pace, while taking a brief moment to pause for one minute.

When your mind is devoid of thoughts and your body is in a state of serenity, direct your attention towards your physical being.

Please position one of your hands on your abdominal region, while placing the other hand on your chest area.

Allow yourself to be receptive to the current of affirmative energy that we have cultivated throughout this endeavor; sense it permeating from within your heart to every inch of your being.

Ensure that you thoroughly evaluate the presence of any obstructions or impediments impeding the smooth circulation of energy within your physical being. In the event that such obstructions are identified, concentrate your energy towards those areas until they are completely eradicated.

Now, I kindly request you to channel that energy externally, directing it into the room. Allow it to encompass the entire space.

Upon attaining the capacity to perceive the palpable presence of the dynamic force encompassing your surroundings, I kindly request that you delve into the recesses of your inner being, seeking solace in your sanctuary. Should you desire, you may employ your preferred term to expedite your arrival.

Experience the sense of security and tranquility; you wield authority in this domain.

Examine your current physical state and become attuned to the sensations in your body. Envision each individual component, commencing with your lower extremities, then progress upward through your lower limbs, subsequently reaching your spinal column and upper torso, eventually descending to your upper limbs and digits.

Place your hands upon your heart and abdomen, acknowledging the fortitude and endurance displayed by your physical being.

Now, I kindly request that you allocate a short period of time to express profound love and sincere appreciation to each and every component of your physical being, acknowledging their invaluable contribution in leading you to this present moment, triumphing over numerous challenges encountered along your journey, and summoning unwavering resilience and optimistic sentiments toward future endeavors.

Subsequently, redirect your focus towards your breath, engaging in three deliberate and measured inhalations and exhalations. Kindly allow me a moment to collect my thoughts.

Once you have completed the task, envision yourself once more within your secure environment, encompassed by the individuals who hold affection and exhibit encouragement towards you in your existence.

Observe the countenance of each individual, scrutinize them deliberately.

Recognize the actions they have taken that have had a positive impact on your daily life.

Acknowledge and commemorate all individuals and their affection; demonstrate love and appreciation towards each individual, allowing their deeds to radiate within you at the present moment.

Experience the solace derived from affection that is wholeheartedly bestowed and reciprocated; grant yourself a brief respite to relish in this sensation as you partake in three additional deliberate breaths, allowing for gradual inhalation and exhalation. Kindly allow me a moment of pause.

I would now request you to mentally conjure up images of those mundane material possessions which elicit a sense of gratitude in your daily existence.

Mentally envisage each individual, clearly picturing the comfort and convenience they bestow upon your daily existence.

Devote a brief period to acknowledge the contributions of these objects to your life, and subsequently express your profound affection and appreciation for each one.

Once you have completed the task, redirect your focus towards your breathing. Take the initiative to perform three deep breaths in a gradual manner, inhaling and exhaling at a slow pace. (Followed by a brief period of silence.)

Now, I kindly request that you allocate a short period of time to consciously observe your secure environment and absorb its elements.

Do any trees or plants exist within that vicinity? Are you able to perceive any fauna?

Observe the heavens to ascertain whether the sun is currently radiating its light, determine the presence or absence of clouds, and take note of any discernible movements of air.

Immerse yourself in the magnificence of the natural world; become one with its essence.

Now, extend your heartfelt affection, compassion, and appreciation to every sentient being inhabiting this planet, for their invaluable support and contribution to your existence.

Direct positive healing energy towards the Earth, in order to facilitate its rejuvenation and foster its optimal state of health.

Please recognize the significance of the natural elements in your existence: bestow your blessings upon Fire, Water, Earth, Air, Weather, Light, and Darkness. Be grateful for their constant presence in your life, and open yourself to what they give you.

Achieve unity with every element and allow their encompassing presence.

Direct your focus towards your breathing once more, and proceed to take three deliberate breaths, engaging in slow inhalation and exhalation. Allow me a moment's respite.

Now, kindly allocate a brief period to vividly imagine and encompass within your mind's eye, your clandestine sanctuary, together with the myriad entities, artefacts, encounters, and organic constituents presently enveloping you.

Allow the boundless well of your positive energy to emanate from the depths of your being, cascading seamlessly through your core and extending gracefully into the conduits of your hands, permeating and saturating the entire expanse of your surroundings.

Observe as the illumination encompasses all, obliterating every trace of darkness and causing all to radiate.

Express profound affection and appreciation, and experience their reciprocation.

Recognize the extraordinary fortune and abundance that you possess in your life, for which you should express profound gratitude.

Express gratitude for the love and assistance bestowed upon you on a daily basis.

Now, please allocate a brief duration to immerse yourself in these feelings of affection and appreciation.

Recite your selected word silently in your thoughts three times to encapsulate all of these sentiments within yourself and brace yourself for the forthcoming encounter on the morrow.

Direct your focus once again onto your breathing, engaging in the act of taking three deep breaths once more, proceeding with a deliberate and gradual inhalation and exhalation. (Please wait momentarily.)

Grant yourself authorization at this moment to depart from your revered place, carrying all the affection and optimistic sentiments along with you.

Experience the vital force emanating from the contact between your palms and allow it to permeate your entire being, gradually reintegrating you into the present moment.

Direct your attention to the present moment, allowing your awareness to focus on the rhythm of your heartbeat, the sensation of the floor beneath you, and the pressure exerted by your hands resting on your heart and abdomen.

Gain a heightened awareness of the auditory and olfactory stimuli present within the room you currently occupy, as well as your own presence within its confines.

Please allow yourself a brief period of time to compose yourself. Once you feel prepared, please proceed to open your eyes.

Inhale deeply three times and subsequently rise, proceeding to energetically tap your feet against the ground.

Please perform this action for a brief duration in order to reestablish your sense of groundedness.

Congratulations, you have successfully concluded today's segment of this program focused on cultivating a mindset of positivity and attaining emotional liberation.

We extend our warm welcome to all who have joined us for the penultimate installment of this transformative expedition dedicated to fostering optimistic attitudes and reclaiming emotional liberation. Today, you will be presented with a series of uplifting affirmations pertaining to your future. They will bolster your assurance and self-worth, equipping you with preparedness to confront the opportunities and challenges that lie ahead.

Prior to commencing, it is advised to ready oneself for the forthcoming encounter by engaging in an exercise that entails clearing one's energy and establishing a grounding state. This simple technique is proposed:

Creative Visualization

How to Construct Objects Through Visualization

Creative visualization is a cognitive process that leverages the power of mental imagery to shape one's perceived reality. Arguably, the most crucial component to acquire proficiency in is the utilization of visualization relaxation techniques within this system. Engaging in activities that promote mental relaxation significantly alleviates psychological strain and exhaustion, thereby profoundly benefiting an individual's overall mental and physical well-being.

The utilization of innovative visualization techniques can equally contribute to an individual's attainment of success and prosperity. However, the absence of exceptional mental and physical well-being diminishes the significance of these qualities for the aspiring individual. Furthermore, it can be inferred that individuals who achieve favorable mental and physical well-being through the practice of visualization relaxation methods will ultimately attain material prosperity.

Regardless of whether individuals are consciously aware or not, they all employ techniques of creative visualization. It is a widely recognized principle acknowledged in every major religion and philosophical tradition. In the sacred text of Christianity, Jesus proclaimed, 'One shall harvest in accordance with what one sows.' In the Hindu faith, this principle is referred to as the law of karma. In the context of this discourse, it is asserted by the principle of creative visualization that one's thoughts or mental imagery directly influence the realization of one's desires or objectives.

Utilizing innovative mental imagery strategies can facilitate enhanced achievements in an individual's professional trajectory, encompassing aspects such as establishing employment, securing a job opportunity, or attaining career advancement along with potential salary increments. One can employ these identical methods to cultivate companionships or establish a romantic connection. Each individual possesses the ability to generate any desired outcome or requirement, provided that it is done in an appropriate manner.

When employed accurately, the strategic utilization of creative visualization techniques possesses the potential to engender a significant and beneficial influence upon not only our own lives but also the lives of those with whom we interact. Nonetheless, the utilization of these very powers can yield unfavorable consequences within our lives should we opt to exploit them through motivations that are self-serving and harbor negative dispositions towards others. Therefore, it is imperative that the individual adheres to the fundamental spiritual principles.

For instance, it is imperative to utilize a portion of one's resources in an altruistic fashion. In addition to our tangible possessions, this encompasses our intellectual and spiritual affluence also. The act of bestowing leads us to acquire even more substantial benefits than those we possessed previously. Arguably, the significance of creative visualization techniques that can be derived from this aspect is unparalleled. That is, we will receive an excess amount beyond our potential utilization. This indicates that instead of squandering these priceless and esteemed resources by hoarding, we assume the obligation to propagate our happiness and enhance the world in which we reside. This phenomenon will have a transformative impact on both our environmental surroundings and our lived experiences.

Effective Visualization Methods for Achieving Desired Outcomes

Foremost amidst these straightforward visualization techniques is to attain a serene state of mind. In order to facilitate effective visualization, it is imperative to attain a state of relaxation and mental tranquility.

However, for the majority of individuals, this seemingly straightforward process proves to be quite challenging upon initial attempts to visualize. Frequently, our minds operate at maximum capacity, handling numerous tasks and an onslaught of thoughts and concerns.

There exists a multitude of activities to engage in... There are a plethora of matters to address... so many worries... Engaged in perpetual multitasking, constantly striving to maintain control amidst numerous responsibilities.

Visualization serves as our refuge from the fast-paced and arduous nature of our modern lifestyles. It serves as a tranquil sanctuary amidst a tumultuous world. With the application of these effective visualization techniques, one can swiftly attain a state of liberation and tranquility, countering the overwhelming influx of mental and physical stimuli. A mere allocation of a brief period would suffice to unwind and rejuvenate your physical, mental, and spiritual state.

Visualization provides relief. You are no longer faced with being pulled in multiple directions, striving to multitask or resolve various pressing matters.

119

Upon achieving the art of calming one's mind, the turbulent clash of conflicting thoughts and demands ceases to persist.

Upon reaching this transcendental state, endeavor to envision your desired objectives, thereby facilitating a return to the designated trajectory. When you are able to calm your thoughts and redirect your focus away from unwanted matters, there exists no factor capable of pulling you down. You enjoy absolute freedom, devoid of any obstacles or constraints imposed by external circumstances, engagements, obligations, stressors, or anxieties. It is complete euphoria, accessible to you whenever you can engage in a few moments of introspection.

Here are straightforward visualization steps to facilitate the attainment of tranquility, lucidity, and unwavering concentration on something of profound desire:

1. Seek out a serene environment in which you can unwind and turn your focus inward.

2. Make yourself comfortable. Wear loose-fitting clothes. Select a seating arrangement that offers adequate comfort during the intended duration of visualization.

3. Close your eyes. Relax. Inhale deeply several times to promote a sense of relaxation. While inhaling, collect the air as a form of vital energy, and as you exhale, envision releasing any and all thoughts that enter your mind.

4. Direct your attention solely towards your breath for a brief duration. Maintain focus on your breath while releasing any conflicting thoughts.

5. As you observe the manifestation of alternative thoughts, merely relinquish them as you exhale. Bestow any degree of consideration upon them, and you

inadvertently grant those thoughts a significant amount of vitality.

6. After liberating your mind, direct your attention towards a desired outcome that you genuinely aspire to manifest. Concentrate on nothing else. Clear your mind of any other thoughts. The objective for you in this process is to maintain a state of relaxation and visualize yourself already possessing your goal.

7. After meticulously envisioning your objective and experiencing its tangible essence in your existence, merely entrust it to the realm of the Universe. Do not develop any emotional or excessive attachment towards it. Visualize it. Accept it as yours. And release it.

What you are essentially accomplishing through this process is eliciting the involvement of your subconscious mind and the universal forces to provide you with assistance. The greater frequency with which one engages in visualization renders it increasingly effortless to attain a state of tranquility, wherein one's imaginative faculties assume control to manifest a spiritual blueprint representing one's desires and aspirations.

You may discover it more convenient to engage with a guided visualization CD. Frequently, the accompanying background music and the calming tone of the narrator facilitate the attainment of a profound meditative state, especially during the initial stages. You are subsequently directed to vividly imagine your objective precisely as intended.

You may obtain whatever you desire. By adhering to these straightforward visualization techniques, you can effortlessly harness the enchantment at your disposal whenever you so desire.

The more promptly you commence, the faster you attain absolute mastery over your fate.

The Manifestation of the Subconscious Mind

Up to this point, it is possible that you have come to recognize that your subconscious mind has the potential to assume the role of your most compliant servant. And you have the ability to bring about numerous positive outcomes in your life. This segment of your cerebral cortex is commonly denoted as a "supreme exemplification facilitator." It possesses the capability to organize elements within your existence, albeit contingent upon adopting a positive vibrational state. A highly effective approach to manifesting is to achieve a state of tranquil mindfulness

124

by engaging in meditation. It unquestionably aids in the process of visualizing and regulating one's emotions.

I hold a strong conviction that our subconscious mind serves as a spiritual essence, or alternatively, it can serve as a conduit to the essence of the soul. Each individual possesses a subconscious mind, a concept that you may have previously encountered, albeit possibly without fully contemplating the nature and potential capabilities of the subconscious mind. There are numerous actions that are executed subconsciously, devoid of conscious contemplation. These activities are acquired at a tender age and subsequently assimilated into the realm of the subconscious mind.

To provide an illustration, consider the scenario where you commence your journey by walking. As an individual begins to engage in the act of walking at a tender age, they gradually become accustomed to the task, improving their abilities over time. Consequently, this task becomes ingrained within their subconscious mind. You need not dwell on this matter any longer; simply proceed with action. Similarly to swimming, driving, and breathing. We possess inherent, pre-determined tasks that are consistently performed by individuals during the course of their lives, similar to a baby's innate abilities such as respiration, nursing, and expressing emotional needs through crying in order to garner attention.

The subconscious mind possesses the capacity to govern a multitude of aspects within your existence, such as the regulation of all primary organs within your physical being. It accomplishes this without necessitating your explicit request. Consider an additional instance involving a pregnant female individual. She is not burdened with contemplation of the developing fetus within her; she does not ponder the timing of when she must commence lactation. It just happens. These represent the primary operations carried out by the subconscious mind, with which you are endowed and which encompass a multitude of functionalities. Nevertheless, it possesses a multitude of capabilities surpassing mere routine tasks that are often overlooked and treated as commonplace.

Conceptualize yourself as embodying two distinct strata, for the context of this discussion - you constitute a cognizant intellect, and simultaneously, an underlying subconscious intellect. The sentient mind is operative within you on a daily basis. Typically, it performs singular tasks exclusively; it encompasses your current thought process, serving as the ultimate arbiter and determiner. It is the individual occupying the position of driver.

The subconscious mind, on the other hand, represents the innermost essence of oneself, operating beyond conscious deliberation as a subordinate entity to the conscious mind. It carries out the instructions provided by the user. You issue commands to it, and it will execute them. If one remains in a perpetual state of worry, their subconscious mind will persistently reiterate the same concerns. It readily complies with the instructions provided.

The subconscious mind holds the power to bring about manifestations in your life. Your rational mind has the capacity to influence and direct your subconscious thoughts. There exists a phenomenon known as the inverse impact, wherein the conscious mind becomes inundated with apprehension, subsequently instructing the subconscious to harbor fear rather than engage in the desired task.

For instance, in the scenario where one intends to deliver a speech before a sizable audience, if their conscious mind is consumed by fear due to its limited capacity to handle multiple tasks simultaneously. The prevailing fear supersedes all other considerations, and your subconscious mind assumes control, compelling you to surrender to anxiety. Consequently, your body becomes a willing servant, responding with numerous physiological reactions that consume your attention.

If you were to adopt a state of relaxation, relinquishing control, and placing trust in the vast intelligence of your subconscious mind, then you would be capable of delivering the speech devoid of any trepidation. In order to achieve this, particularly when faced with the task of delivering a speech to a large audience, it is necessary to relinquish the perpetual apprehension that initially plagues you. And relinquish any deliberate concerns or whatsoever.

This phenomenon is characterized by a contrasting endeavor, wherein one experiences an intense sense of apprehension, and paradoxically, the more one fears something, the more it induces a state of mental blankness. In order to achieve success in these endeavors, it is imperative to utilize one's subconscious mind, as it is the repository of authentic memories and innate abilities. Prior to undertaking this task, I hereby delegate authority to you to assume control and decision-making responsibilities regarding its execution."

Allow your conscious mind to recede, as your subconscious mind flawlessly attends to the task. It possesses an inherent understanding of the appropriate course of action. That serves as an exemplary instance: when operating a motor vehicle, one may come to the unexpected realization that, after approximately 40 minutes of driving, the recollection of the journey becomes hazy, attributable to the vigilance of one's subconscious mind during the excursion.

Under such circumstances, it is likely that your conscious mind was preoccupied with various matters, while your subconscious mind remained perpetually alert. It remains constantly awake and in perpetual presence. It remains alert even during the late hours of the night when you are in a state of deep slumber. Kindly request your conscious mind to temporarily abdicate its position. By harnessing the power of emotions and employing the technique of repetitive affirmations, you can communicate to your subconscious faculties, allowing them to assume control. You may convincingly convey statements such as "I entrust you to navigate the path," "I empower you to deliver this address," or "I grant you permission to engage with these unfamiliar individuals." As you surrender control and detach from any exertion, your subconscious mind will seamlessly execute these tasks.

A frequently cited scenario involves finding oneself in the company of an individual while anticipating the approach of an acquaintance, with the awareness that an introduction will be necessary upon their arrival. Due to the apprehension and concern that pervades your thoughts, it is imperative that you retain their name so as to properly acquaint them with your acquaintance. The conscious mind, overwhelmed by fear, is incapable of performing the multiple tasks that the subconscious mind naturally handles.

Therefore, if one becomes increasingly anxious and apprehensive about the approach of this individual and harbors concerns about potentially forgetting their name, it is likely that such apprehension will lead to the anticipated outcome of forgetting. Conversely, by ceasing to worry and adopting a relaxed state, thereby allowing the subconscious mind to operate freely, one can miraculously recall the person's name. Therefore, it is imperative that you maintain mastery over your conscious mind. In the current era, we find ourselves increasingly preoccupied and burdened; a worrisome state of affairs, as the thoughts and concerns occupying our conscious mind have a profound impact on our subconscious mind. The big strong slave. It is a slave.

If you consistently indulge in excessive anxiety and stress, these detrimental thoughts become deeply ingrained within your subconscious mind, which subsequently becomes subservient to them. All information is assimilated into your consciousness, and whatever is assimilated will subsequently materialize. It will effectively resolve the matter for you. Therefore, if you are concerned about the timely completion of that project, it is infeasible to meet the deadline.

The aforementioned factors are transmitting messages to your subconscious, which in turn will endeavor to ensure that you are unable to complete the task punctually and will strive to lead you towards failure in the said endeavor. If you maintain a sense of assurance and transmit solely affirmative messages to the subconscious, affirming that "everything will be all right, I am capable of achieving this," the subconscious mind will attune itself to your commands and act accordingly. And suddenly, your positive aspirations will be materialized. Bear in mind that the subliminal facet of the mind remains functional and relevant in the contemporary context.

You consistently provide instructions in the present tense, which can occasionally present challenges, as there is no distinction between the future or past within the realm of the subconscious mind. Therefore, it is essential to provide clear instructions in the present. Your past beliefs inevitably give rise to a continuous succession of additional challenges. Your previous thought processes have had a profound impact on both your current circumstances and your upcoming prospects.

For instance, in the event that you consistently encountered a parental upbringing wherein you were persistently subjected to criticism, being labeled as inadequate, useless, and incompetent, the question of "why do you possess such unfavorable qualities?" may arise. Why do you exhibit such mischievous behavior? These messages become embedded in your subconscious mind, continuously reinforcing the notion that you possess little value and have no potential for success. Consequently, your actions and behaviors align with this self-fulfilling prophecy, ensuring that you do not excel or achieve any worthwhile accomplishments. It is imperative that you make an effort to discern these underlying causes.

Hence, engaging in regression or deep meditation allows individuals to revisit the moments when those remarks were made to them. You may attempt to engage in dialogue with your previous self and impart upon them that the aforementioned situation did not, in fact, occur. It was unjust and I recommend releasing any resentment towards it. To convey to the latent inner self that internalized those unfavorable messages, it is imperative to instill faith in the evolved version of oneself, trusting that the contemporary self is fully capable of assuming control.

Therefore, it is necessary for you to uncover and examine those prior convictions and ingrained messages that were imprinted in your impressionable psyche. Thoroughly acquaint yourself with them and rectify the situation promptly by gaining a comprehensive understanding of oneself. After acknowledging and addressing the personality traits that have been deeply ingrained within your subconscious mind, you can then bestow your confidence upon the reformed version of yourself, empowering it to assume control.

Consequently, the updated iteration of yourself has the capability to generate a novel program for your subconscious mind, wherein fresh signals supersede and supplant antiquated ones. By surpassing your pre-existing beliefs, you have the potential to cultivate an enhanced or potentially unparalleled embodiment of yourself. It is simply a matter of perception!

For instance, if the objective is to achieve weight loss and attain a more slender physique, the focus should be on striving to become slimmer. You must possess resolute convictions regarding your desire to attain a slim physique. Establish expectations that are sufficiently robust to materialize them in actuality. Exhibit sufficient self-assurance in order to achieve unequivocal success in your aspirations. Envision yourself achieving success in your aspiration to attain a slim physique. Develop a sufficient level of self-assurance in attaining a slender physique and vividly envision the actualization of this desired outcome.

It is essential to envision that all of these events are presently unfolding. Furthermore, this particular attribute of the subconscious mind also results in another significant phenomenon, which remains imperceptible to the subconscious. The conscious mind possesses the ability to perceive, deliberate, and transmit directives to the subconscious mind unbeknownst to one's awareness.

Therefore, the subconscious mind lacks visual perception and can solely perceive information dictated by the conscious mind. It possesses the ability to perceive fictitious entities. Your cognitive faculties possess the volition to enact actions; they perceive, deliberate, and possess the volition to actualize any desired outcome. The subconscious mind possesses solely the faculty of imagination.

It is guided by one's imagination, incapable of discerning between actual events and mere figments of the mind. Hence, the significance of visualization and imagination arises, as the subconscious mind lacks the ability to discern distinctions. If an unfavorable event occurs in your life and leaves a lasting impact on your subconscious, causing persistent negative emotions, envisioning positive occurrences can effectively influence your subconscious and ultimately improve your overall well-being.

By engaging in the faculties of imagination and visualization, one can conceive any desired outcome, whereby the subconscious mind diligently endeavors to manifest it. Thus, one can easily envision or mentally conjure a vivid scenario, akin to encountering an individual with whom they share an intense romantic connection. You have quite the imagination regarding the prospect of meeting them. It is imperative to employ the power of visualization by cultivating a sense of expectation, profound desire, and unwavering confidence.

At present, the subconscious mind is incapable of discerning the distinction between actuality and imagination. It feigns attainment of the aforementioned goal. Over time, it ensures its manifestation. This must be demonstrated in accordance with the principles of the Law of Attraction. Therefore, it is vital to be mindful that your subconscious mind assumes a hierarchical relationship, wherein it diligently ensures the materialization of your aspirations. This meditation technique facilitates enhanced empowerment through the practice of visualization.

Configure it with optimistic sentiments to enhance its functionality. From a scientific standpoint, it is hypothesized that this phenomenon is associated with a particular region of the brain that is not yet fully comprehended, and that it can be influenced or modulated through programming techniques. However, I hold a strong conviction that it originates from a component of the psyche known as the higher self. You possess elevated transcendence due to its exceptional capabilities.

Establish a line of communication with your subconscious mind, thereby inducing a process of reprogramming to effectively materialize more favorable circumstances and foster a higher quality of life for your own self. Attain your desires and experience enhanced well-being, while discovering increased joy and tranquility from within. The subconscious mind truly possesses the answer. "It pertains to the enhanced, robust self, while the conscious mind solely attends to external aspects of life and facilitates decision-making. Nevertheless, you possess the ability to direct the subconscious mind."

Expert Advice - To maintain a strong link between your conscious and subconscious mind, it is essential to consistently reinforce positive thoughts through repetition. The sooner you will materialize is directly proportional to the degree of positivity in your mindset.

Remarkable Visualization Strategies to Effectively Transform Your Life

Positive thoughts yield positive outcomes, while negative thoughts result in unfavorable consequences. Take a moment to envision yourself as a gardener within your thoughts. Consider the types of fruits you would choose to cultivate. It is important to keep in mind that a prosperous horticulturist purposefully nurtures beneficial seeds that will eventually blossom into the desired future.

Hence, it is of paramount importance for you to engage in the daily reprogramming of your mindset. The construction of your personal reality depends on how you perceive and discern your surroundings. In fact, you do not base your actions on your factual understanding, but rather on your interpretation of that understanding. You consistently experience and conduct yourself based not on objective reality, but rather on the subjective mental image you hold of reality.

By engaging in visualization, it is possible to alter one's perception of oneself and the surrounding environment. You may subsequently engage in honing the skills in which you aspire to excel. This implies that your thought processes determine your actions, self-worth, and overall sense of contentment.

Exercise#1: Simple memory visualization

Identify a serene location wherein you can unwind and allocate a period of twenty minutes daily for the purpose of engaging in visualization exercises. Ensure that you are devoid of any manner of interruption. Please shut your eyes and engage in deep breathing to initiate the relaxation of your mind.

Envision yourself suspended at great heights within the vast expanse of the atmosphere. There is no necessity for you to visually perceive anything. Envision oneself soaring, levitating, being held aloft in the atmosphere. Next, envisage a perspective from above, gazing upon residential dwellings and their rooftops.

Attempt to mentally envision your abode. How would it appear when viewed from the perspective of the atmosphere? Envision a scenario in which you descend leisurely, finding yourself positioned outside your residence's main entrance. Subsequently, envision yourself approaching the aforementioned entity. Can you observe the hue, composition, components of the doorway, transparent surface, or the mechanism used for grasping?

Upon closer examination of the door, ascertain the true level of precision you possess. Once you become accustomed to the practice of visualization, you can proceed to replicate this exercise by envisioning the opening of the door, entering, and subsequently envisaging floating through each of the rooms.

Exercise #2: Visualizing the act of consuming a lemon

Un-wind your mind. Please envision the presence of a basket filled with lemons in close proximity to your current location. While still in the realm of imagination, select a fully matured yellow lemon. Perceive the tangible mass when clutching it. Delicately glide your fingertips across the sleek and lustrous peel of that lemon. Please attempt to perceive the indented surface. Elevate the lemon to your olfactory organ and engage in the act of inhaling the scent of the lemon. Gently and gradually incise the lemon, revealing the scantily exposed pale yellow pulp.

I am confident that you will observe the juice steadily flowing out, resulting in the pervasive diffusion of the lemon fragrance in your immediate vicinity. Cut the lemon into small sections and take a bite of one piece, allowing the juice to flow over your palate. Indeed, your salivary glands will be stimulated. Consequently, it can be inferred that the physical reactions of the body are intricately connected to the psychological state of the mind.

Task #3: Visualization of Reflections in Water

Make an effort to observe your own reflection in a pool of water. Ensure that your reflection is clearly visible in the water. Now, envision yourself positioned behind your own self, observing your reflection within the pool.

In one's imagination, position oneself to the side while simultaneously observing the reflection in the water and the profile of one's face. Envision yourself gradually receding and observing your own reflection in the pool, subsequently picturing yourself distancing from the water and engaging in a distinct activity.

Exercise #4: Hypnosis induction

Comfortably sit down. Please calm your mind and subsequently shut your eyes. Envision a chalkboard, azure heavens, or sandy shore. Envision a large circular shape, followed by the inscribing of the letter "a" within its bounds. After a few minutes have elapsed, it is subsequently removed and replaced with the letter "b".

Envision a scenario wherein the action of writing and erasing seamlessly intertwines in a perpetuating sequence, following the orderly progression of the alphabet. This will induce an unfamiliar sensation as you are now immersed in a hypnotic state induced by these alphabetical characters. This signifies that visualization can be regarded as a variant of self-hypnosis that is founded upon affirmations.

Exercise #5: Envision the process of maturing

Envision the process of maturing from infancy to adolescence. Observe every element of your appearance, encompassing your choice of attire, the style of your hair, and the smoothness of your skin. Envision the act of traveling to the educational institution. Envision yourself as an author diligently chronicling the journey of that adolescent as they navigate the complexities of maturation. Make an effort to perceive from the perspective of the writer. Visualize yourself observing the writer's gaze upon you, both directly and within the realm of mental imagery. Envision observing facial expressions on the notepad.

Task #6: Engage in mental imagery of participating in a competitive running event

Engage in positioning oneself at the conclusion point of a competitive running event. Direct your focus towards the ongoing progress of the race. Continue observing as you approach nearer. Remain stationary as the visual expands. Subsequently, provide an analysis on the performance of the runner. Provide an analysis regarding their respiration and perspiration. Continue observing as the image progressively expands in size; you will be able to gaze directly into her gaze.

Exercise #7: Engage in the act of envisioning a scenario where one gazes through a pane of glass

Endeavor to envision yourself engaged in a task within the confines of your own residence. Regardless of your physical location, whether it be a confined space or an open area, observe with scrutiny through a minute aperture. The only thing that is visible is a solitary hand. After a brief duration, the aperture expands, thereby allowing for an increased perspective. In a short span of time, the aperture expands and progressively enlarges, enabling you to perceive your own reflection and observe your actions.

Observe the core from a standing position, thereby enhancing the level of challenge. Observe yourself engaged in the task, with your image being mirrored, thereby allowing for simultaneous contemplation of both reflections.

Exercise #8: Envision the motion of a fluttering flag

Envision an image depicting a national flag. Visualize the presence of the flag on a pole or atop a building in one's mind's eye. Consider the visual impact that will ensue when a gust of wind is present. Attempt to amplify the force of the wind to a level sufficient for the movement of objects such as trees, grass, and airborne debris.

Exercise #9: Input the statement

You have currently assumed a position of concentration. Envision a particular issue or event, and permit your thoughts to wander across various facets until a sense of unease or an emotional response within your physical being is felt. It is highly likely that you will experience a sense of anxiety or discomfort, leading to your departure from that state.

Please take a brief respite and subsequently replicate the identical course of action. Eventually, you will come to the realization that a portion of your being has grown tranquil, while any traces of negative emotions have dissipated.

Exercise #10: Examine the condition by means of visualization.

Envision yourself engaging with a particular visual representation. Please introspect and consider what would be the optimal condition for that image. Allow your thoughts the opportunity to explore various possibilities. Witness alterations in hue, form, and various transformations. After a certain duration has elapsed, there will be no alteration evident within it.

At this juncture, a realization dawns upon you: "What was the purpose and utility of this entity? For what reason was it designed?" Allow your mind to provide you with the answer. Once you reach a stage where verbalization dominates your thinking, you will have departed from the intended state. Return to the matter at hand, and in the event that the answer arises effortlessly from your subconscious in such a state, it will impart a profound understanding of how you consciously navigate your choices in various aspects of your life.

How Mind Works?

Have you ever pondered the nature and mechanistic functioning of the human mind? The brain undergoes division not only based on its functions, but also by the state of awareness, specifically comprising the conscious and subconscious aspects of the mind. Kindly be aware that this does not imply possessing dual perspectives/minds.

The cognitive faculties of the human brain enable rational deliberation, logical comprehension, critical assessment, determination, and subsequent implementation of a course of action. Presented below are four essential functions attributed to our conscious minds:
1. Identify
2. Comparison
3. Analyze
4. Determine the precise course of action in response to the provided information.

The conscious mind commenced its activity at the age of three, assuming control of logical functions. As we mature, our conscious mind will assist us in refraining from making any unnecessary alterations, employing a filtering mechanism known as the critical factor. The critical factor consistently evaluates incoming information by harnessing the inherent database within the subconscious mind.

The subconscious mind is inclined to internalize any information or beliefs that are imparted by the conscious mind. The programs are consistently regarded as truths by the subconscious mind. Let us now examine the programs that are stored within our subconscious mind.

1. Habits

All manner of habits, whether they be favorable or unfavorable, are intricately ingrained within the recesses of our subconscious faculties.

2 Emotions

The subconscious mind will elicit the specific emotions that are provoked by the specific memories, events, or experiences.

3 Long-Term Memories

All occurrences are impeccably documented within the recesses of our subliminal consciousness, although they elude our conscious recollection. We have the ability to utilize hypnosis as a means of delving into these memories.

4. Personality
Through the amalgamation of our various experiences and responses, our subconscious mind constructs our individuality, shaping us into the individuals we are today.

5. Intuition
Due to the presence of unacknowledged data or information in the conscious mind, the subconscious mind endeavours to establish communication with the conscious mind through the utilization of intuition. For instance, to communicate information that eludes conscious awareness, to relay potential hazards, or to forecast positive or negative events. The intuition may manifest itself in the form of a physiological response, a vision during sleep, or an emotive sensation.

6. Creativity

Creativity encompasses the intellectual capacity to transform abstract concepts and aspirations into tangible manifestations. The subconscious mind will persistently endeavor to accomplish the objectives that have been ingrained within, whether they are constructive or detrimental in nature.

7. Perception

Perception entails our perspective on the world. The manifestations that arise are the result of prior knowledge that has been imbued with established patterns.

8. Belief and Value

Belief is the cognitive construct through which individuals ascertain and internalize their perception of truth. Value refers to the things that hold significance in one's perspective. Our belief systems and core values are fundamentally influenced by our perception when confronted with specific circumstances. Belief and value are perspectives that are inherently subjective, derived through a synthesis of our personal experiences, knowledge, and aspirations.

The subconscious mind will persistently execute or carry out the aforementioned programs regardless of circumstances. Once the program becomes integrated within our subconscious mind, regardless of the circumstances, it will persistently operate. Upon the implementation of a new program to replace the current one.

Furthermore, it is imperative that I address a total of 8 fundamental principles pertaining to the mind. Ever since psychology emerged as an empirical discipline in the mid-19th century, we have made considerable strides in comprehending the intricacies of the human mind.

The field of neuroscience, which is experiencing rapid advancements, is facilitating the linkage between the brain and its influence on cognition and behavior. As our understanding of the workings of our remarkable brain deepens, we gain enhanced insight into the underlying causes of our cognitive processes, emotional experiences, and behavioral patterns. The ensuing are eight principles of cognition that have been meticulously refined over an extended duration and imparted within the discipline of hypnotherapy.

Principle 1: Each cognitive notion or concept elicits a somatic response.
One's cognitive processes have a notable impact on one's physical well-being. The mind and body represent two interdependent facets of a cohesive whole. The psyche possesses the capability to induce illness or confer a sense of well-being. Anger elicits an elevation in adrenaline levels, while fear and anxiety provoke an accelerated heart rate, thereby potentially contributing to cardiovascular complications. Additionally, it may assume a corporeal manifestation

through the emergence of ulcers, headaches, or other bodily symptoms.

Concepts and principles that possess significant emotional resonance have a profound impact on our psyche, ultimately assuming an autonomous existence within our subconscious. Upon acceptance, these ideas and beliefs persistently elicit a consistent physiological response. In order to eradicate or modify persistent adverse bodily responses, it is imperative to delve into the subconscious realm and alter the notions and convictions that are accountable for such reactions.

Second principle: There is a tendency for anticipated outcomes to materialize.
Our cognition reacts to internal or external mental representations, whether they are self-generated or derived from external stimuli. The mental image that is forged becomes the guiding plan, and the subconscious mind diligently employs all accessible

resources, strategies, and techniques to manifest it into reality.

Therefore, it is imperative to consistently uphold a optimistic mindset, for our thoughts have the power to shape our ultimate reality. The significance of your mental state cannot be overstated when it comes to achieving success in various domains of life, such as your well-being, finances, professional pursuits, athletic endeavors, and interpersonal relationships.

Principle 3: Within the realm of the mind, the potency of imagination eclipses that of rationality.

The faculty of creative thinking serves as the communicative medium through which the unconscious psyche expresses itself. Imagination has a propensity to triumph over reason. Concepts that are infused with intense emotional fervor, encompassing sentiments such as anger, animosity, trepidation, and even affection, present formidable challenges when attempting to subject them to rational modification.

Navigating across a floor-mounted plank measuring 6 inches in width poses little difficulty for the majority of individuals. As the elevation of the board increases by 20 feet, the task of traversing it becomes arduous and unattainable for the majority of individuals. Why? The distinction lies in the strength of imagination, the perpetual envisioning of the potential consequence wherein even a single misstep could lead to a deadly outcome.

Once more, it should be emphasized that imagination serves as the mode of communication for the subconscious mind. To surmount any obstacles, it is imperative that your imagination and reasoning faculties operate in tandem.

Guideline 4: Simultaneously holding contradictory notions is not permissible. The human intellect is incapable of maintaining two contradictory beliefs concurrently. A significant number of individuals endeavor to simultaneously maintain two contradictory notions. This phenomenon is commonly referred to as cognitive dissonance in the field of psychology.

As an example, it is inconceivable to perceive oneself simultaneously as both attractive and unattractive, or to simultaneously experience both love and hate towards someone.

An individual may embrace the principle of veracity, yet engage in deceitful conduct. This behavior could potentially find justification through rationalizations such as the following: "It is a common practice among many individuals." "Small falsehoods should not be considered significant." "My personal need outweighs that of others." "I am entitled to a respite." These rationalizations directly contradict the deeper value and belief in maintaining honesty. One could rationalize his actions as being in accordance with nature, however, the act of following a conscious thought that inherently contradicts a deeply ingrained subconscious belief leads to significant psychological distress, thereby exerting a profound influence on one's physical well-being.

Rule number 5 dictates that once an idea has gained acceptance from the subconscious mind, it maintains its state of acceptance until it is superseded by a different idea.

According to psychologists, individuals experience an average of 45,000 to 60,000 thoughts per day. Moreover, the thoughts we currently possess, amounting to approximately 95%, are likely to persist in our cognitive framework over subsequent days and beyond. The rationale behind this is that our beliefs and values system remains constant unless we actively choose to modify it.

The human mind operates by establishing patterns and utilizing shortcuts, thereby enabling the formation of thoughts, habits, and behaviors. The greater our cognitive contemplation of a particular idea, the more we reinforce the neural connections within our cerebral framework, thereby incorporating it into our consciousness. The more persistent the idea you maintain, it will develop into a mindset. This is the manner in which the mindset was shaped, whether for better or worse.